INHALTSVERZEICHNIS
(TABLE OF CONTENTS)

THE 20 FUNNIEST GERMAN WORD CREATIONS   36

DANKESCHÖN! THANK YOU!   **50**

PREFACE

So, you are interested in some fun German idioms? Maybe you are a beginner at German and just want to see what this language has to offer. Or perhaps you are an advanced German speaker and want to spice up your conversation. Whatever your reasoning, this book will be great to get started with for German idioms and word creations and I hope you get some good laughs out of it.

Before publishing this book, most of my students suggested translating the idioms into British and American English, something which I tried to do throughout the book. Also, one of my students suggested recording audio for it (downloadable at learngermanwithanja.com/best-german-expressions-book/)

Finally, I'd just like to say a big thank you to all of my students who inspired me and helped me to shape this book! I really enjoyed writing this book and I couldn't have done any of it without your love, support, and inspiration!

Abbreviations used in the book:

Sth. – something   Sb. – somebody

A NOTE ON PROFANITY

This book uses some adult language (marked with "vulg.") which is unsuitable for young children. However, knowing some of these expressions is nonetheless a dealbreaker for your trip to Germany. It is useful to understand them, but as somebody who is a native speaker, I'm telling you that it's better to not use them until you get a clear understanding of what they mean and when it is appropriate or inappropriate to use them. In the meantime, just have some fun reading about them! ☺

THE 55 BEST GERMAN IDIOMS

With their Meanings, Translations and

Sample Sentences

---

1. ICH GLAUB' MEIN SCHWEIN PFEIFT

Literally: I believe/think my pig is whistling

Meaning: expression of astonishment/surprise; "I think I'm going off my rocker!"

Examples: „Das ist nicht wahr! Ich glaub' mein Schwein pfeift!"
"That's not true! I think I'm going off my rocker!"

„Ich glaub' mein Schwein pfeift! Du bist noch nicht fertig?"
"I can't believe it! You aren't ready yet?"

2. 'NE FLIEGE MACHEN

'ne = eine

Literally: to make a fly

Meaning: 1) demand to go; "Get out of here!"
               2) to leave

Examples: 1) „Mach 'ne Fliege!"
               "Get out of here!"
               2) „Bis morgen, ich mach' 'ne Fliege!" (mach'=
               mache/ 'ne = eine)
               "See you tomorrow, I'm out of here!"

---

3. DIE NASE/DIE SCHNAUZE VOLL HABEN

Literally: to have the nose/snout full

Meaning: to have enough of sth.; "to be fed up with
               something"

Examples: „Ich habe die Nase voll vom Lernen!"
               "I'm fed up with learning!"

               „Es regnet schon seit einer Woche. Ich hab' die
               Schnauze voll!"
               "It's been raining for a week. I've had enough!"

4. Nur Bahnhof verstehen

Literally: to only understand train station

Meaning: to not understand anything; "It's all Greek to me."

Examples: *„Ich verstehe nur Bahnhof!"*
"I don't understand anything at all!"

„Im Unterricht heute habe ich mal wieder nur Bahnhof verstanden."
"The lessons today were once again all Greek to me."

5. DIE KACKE IST AM DAMPFEN (VULG.)

Literally: the shit is steaming

Meaning: "There is trouble going on."; "The shit has hit the fan."

Examples: „Jetzt ist die Kacke am Dampfen."
                "Now the shit has hit the fan."
                „Das gibt Ärger, die Kacke ist richtig am Dampfen."
                "There will be trouble, the shit has hit the fan."

---

6. (DA IST/HIER IST) TOTE HOSE!

Literally: (There is/Here is) dead pants/trousers!

Meaning: something is really boring; "Nothing is going on (here/there)"

Examples: „Auf der Party ist tote Hose."
                "The party is really boring."

                „Ich gehe, hier ist tote Hose!"
                "I'm leaving, nothing's going on here!"

Note: A very similar expression is "Kein Schwein war da!", which literally translates to "No pig was there", meaning "nobody was there." For example:

                „Ich war in der Schule, aber kein Schwein war da."
                "I was at school, but not a single person was there."

"Kein Schwein" can also be used in other phrases (slang!). For example: „Kein Schwein ruft mich an."
                "Not a single person calls me."

7. Das ist mir Wurst

Literally: this is sausage to me

Meaning: I don't care; I don't mind; I couldn't care less

Examples: „Magst du den roten oder blauen Becher?" - „Das ist mir Wurst!"
"Do you like the red or blue cup?" - "I don't care!"

„Er hat eine neue Freundin, aber das ist mir Wurst."
"He's got a new girlfriend, but I couldn't care less."

„Dieses Thema ist mir Wurst."
"I don't care about this topic."

---

8. Jetzt/Da haben wir den Salat!

Literally: Now/There we have the salad

Meaning: to be in a bad/uncomfortable situation; "Now we are in a fine mess!"; "That turned out badly."; "What did I tell you!"

Examples: „Du wolltest ja nicht auf mich hören, da haben wir den Salat!"
"You didn't want to listen to me, now that turned out badly!"

"Ich habe dich davor gewarnt, aber jetzt haben wir den Salat!"
"I warned you, but now we are in a fine mess!"

9. HIER REIN, DA RAUS

(Zum einen Ohr rein, zum anderen raus)

Literally: here in, there out; in one ear and out the other

Meaning: to ignore sth. that was just said; to not listen/care

Examples: *„Was ich sage, geht bei meinem Bruder hier rein und da raus."*
"What I tell my brother goes in one ear and out the other."

„Das geht bei ihm zum einen Ohr rein und zum anderen raus."
"That goes in one ear and out the other."

10. Einen Stock im Arsch haben (vulg.)

Literally: to have a stick in the
             ass/arse

Meaning: to be stuffy,
             humourless/overly formal
             "To have a stick up one's
             ass/arse"

Examples: „Er hat einen Stock im
             Arsch!"
             *"He's got a stick up his
             ass/arse!"*

             „Hat die immer einen
             Stock im Arsch?"
             "Does she always have a stick up her ass/arse?"

---

11. Spinnen

Literally: to "spider" (die Spinne = the spider)
             Note: "spinnen" also means "to spin" or "to yarn"

Meaning: to be crazy, "to be out of one's mind"

Examples: „Ich glaub', ich spinne!"
             "I think, I am out of my mind!"

             „Spinnst du etwa?"
             "Are you insane?"

             „Du spinnst doch!"
             "You are crazy!"

12. Schwein haben

Literally: to have pig

Meaning: to be lucky; "to have a stroke of luck"

Examples: „Schwein gehabt!"
              "That was lucky!"

              „Ich hatte echt Schwein!"
              "I really had a stroke of luck!"

---

13. Schwamm drüber

Literally: sponge over it

Meaning: "Let's forget it!"; "No hard feelings!"

Examples: „Entschuldigung angenommen, Schwamm
              drüber!"
              "Apology accepted, let's forget it!"

              „Es war wohl ein Missverständnis, also Schwamm
              drüber!"
              "That was probably a misunderstanding, so no hard
              feelings!"

              „Schwamm drüber, das muss nicht perfekt sein!"
              "No hard feelings, it doesn't have to be perfect!"

TIP: Instead of "Schwamm drüber", it is also very common to say
"(Das) Macht nichts!" which literally means "that makes nothing",
meaning: "No problem!/ No worries!"

Examples:	„Oh, Entschuldigung!"- „Macht nichts!"
	"Oh, sorry!"- "No problem, never mind!"

„Das macht mir nichts aus!"
"That's not bothering me!"

---

14. ALLES IN BUTTER

Literally:	all in butter
Meaning:	everything's okay
Examples:	„Wie geht es dir?"- „Alles in Butter!"
	"How are you?" - "Everything's okay!"

„Alles in Butter bei dir?"
"Everything going okay for you?"

15. Hummeln im Hintern/im Arsch haben (vulg.)

Literally: to have bumble bees in the butt/ass/arse

Meaning: to be antsy, to be fidgety; "to have ants in the pants"

Examples: *„Er hat Hummeln im Hintern!"*
             "He has ants in his pants!"

             „Hast du immer Hummeln im Arsch?"
             "Are you always so fidgety?"

---

16. Die Sau rauslassen

Literally: to let the sow out

Meaning: to go crazy, to party hard; "To let one's hair down"; "to paint the town red"

Examples: *„Heute lassen wir so richtig die Sau raus auf der Party!"*
             "Today we will go crazy at the party!"

             „Peter hat gestern die Sau rausgelassen."
             "Yesterday, Peter let his hair down."

17. Das ist nicht mein Bier.

Literally: That is not my beer

Meaning: that is none of my business, that is not my problem

Examples: „Ich würde es anders machen, aber das ist nicht mein Bier."
"I would do it differently, but it's none of my business."

„Es gibt Probleme in der Firma, aber das ist nicht mein Bier."
"There are problems in the company but that's not my problem."

„Halt dich da raus, es ist nicht dein Bier!"
"Keep out of it. It's none of your business!"

---

18. Ankotzen - Etwas ist zum Kotzen (vulg.)

Literally: to vomit on - sth. is for vomiting

Meaning: "that pisses sb. off"; to make sb. sick/vomit

Examples: „Das kotzt mich an!"
"That pisses me off!" (lit.: "That vomits on me.")

„Das ist doch zum Kotzen!"
"That makes me sick!"; "That sucks!" (lit.: "That's for vomiting!")

19. Bis der Arzt kommt

Literally: until the doctor comes

Meaning: to continue to do something to the point of excess;
              "until you drop"

Examples: „Wir feiern bis der Arzt kommt."
              "We are going to party until we drop."

              „Heute wird getanzt bis der Arzt kommt."
              "Today we are dancing until the end."

---

20. (Ich glaub') ich fress' 'nen Besen!

((Ich glaube), Ich fresse einen Besen)

Literally: (I believe), I'll devour a broom

Meaning: exclamation of incredulity, surprise; "I'll eat my
              words!";
              "I'll eat my hat/shirt if that is true!"

Examples: „Ich glaub' ich fress' 'nen Besen, wenn das wahr
              ist!"
              "I believe, I'll eat my words, if that's true!"

              „Wenn das stimmt, fress' ich 'nen Besen!" ('nen =
              einen)
              "If that's true, I'll eat my hat/shirt!"

21. (NICHT) ALLE TASSEN IM SCHRANK HABEN

Literally: to (not) have all cups in the cupboard

Meaning: "to have a screw loose"; "to lose one's marbles"

Examples: „Du hast doch nicht alle Tassen im Schrank!"
"You have a screw loose!"

„Hat der nicht alle Tassen im Schrank?"
"Has he lost his marbles?"

---

22. UNTER ALLER SAU

Literally: under all pig

Meaning: really bad, a mess, really lousy

Examples: „Mein Deutsch ist unter aller Sau."
"My German is really lousy."

„Er benimmt sich wieder unter aller Sau!"
"He's behaving really badly again!"

„Die Organisation hier ist unter aller Sau."
"The organization here is a big mess."

23. AM ARSCH DER WELT (VULG.)

Literally: at the ass/arse of the world

Meaning: in the middle of nowhere

Examples: *„Wir sind hier am Arsch der Welt gelandet!"*
"We ended up in the middle of nowhere!"

„Du wohnst echt am Arsch der Welt."
"You really live in the middle of nowhere."

---

24. AUF DEN KEKS/SACK GEHEN (VULG.)

Literally: To go on someone's cookie / To go on someone's balls (der Keks = the cookie; der Sack = bag or testicles/balls)

Meaning: to get on sb.'s nerves

Examples: *„Seine Musik geht mir auf den Keks."*
"His music really gets on my nerves."

„Du gehst mir auf den Sack!" (vulg.)
"You are a pain the ass/arse!"

25. AUS DER HAUT FAHREN

Literally: to drive out of the skin

Meaning: to get very angry; to lose your temper; "To fly off
             the handle"; "to make a fuss"

Examples: „Sie fährt schnell aus der Haut."
             "She loses her temper quickly."

             „Das ist zum Aus-der-Haut-fahren!"
             "That makes me lose my temper!"

             „Warum fährst du immer so schnell aus der Haut?"
             "Why do you always get angry so quickly?"

---

26. KEINEN BOCK HABEN

Literally: not having buck (male goat or sheep/male animal)

Meaning: no motivation, not feeling like doing something

Examples: „Ich hab' keinen Bock auf Arbeit!"
             "I don't feel like working!"

             „Susi hat keinen Bock zu lernen."
             "Susi has no motivation to learn."

27. Sport ist Mord

Literally: sport is murder

Meaning: phrase said ironically by someone who is not
               enjoying (struggling doing) physical activity

Examples: *„Nie wieder joggen! Sport ist Mord!"*
               "No more jogging! Sport is murder!"

               „Alles tut mir weh! Sport ist Mord!"
               "My whole body is hurting! Sport is murder!"

---

28. Das ist zum Mäusemelken!

Literally: I could milk mice because of that!

Meaning: sth. is cumbersome; hardscrabble (without result);
               "It is enough to drive you up the wall."

Examples: *„Er wird es nie verstehen, es ist zum Mäusemelken!"*
               "He will never get it, it's so cumbersome!"

               *„Ich sitze seit Tagen an dieser Präsentation und
               komme nicht weiter! Das ist zum Mäusemelken!"*
               *"I have been sitting on this presentation for days
               without making any progress. It's driving me up the
               wall!"*

29. EINEN VOGEL HABEN

Literally: to have a bird (in the head)

Meaning: to be crazy; "to be nuts"

Examples: „Du hast einen Vogel!"
             "You are nuts!"

             „Hat der 'nen Vogel?" (= "einen Vogel")
             "He is crazy, isn't he?"

30. Alter Schwede!

Literally: old Swede!

Meaning: expression of astonishment; "Gosh!"; "Oh, my
                Goodness!"; "Good grief!"

Examples: „Alter Schwede! Ich glaub es nicht!"
                "Gosh, I can't believe it!"

                „Alter Schwede, das ist nicht wahr!"
                "Good grief, that's not true!"

                „Alter Schwede, hast du das gesehen?"
                "Oh, my Goodness, have you seen this?"

---

31. (Der) Hammer!

Literally: (the) hammer!

Meaning: "Unbelievably awesome!"; "Cool!"; "Off da hook!"

Examples: „Das ist ja der Hammer!"
                "That's off da hook!"

                „Das Meer ist der Hammer!"
                "The ocean is awesome!"

                „Die Party war der Hammer!"
                "The party's been super cool!"

32. Für einen Apfel und ein Ei

Literally: for an apple and an egg

Meaning: something is very cheap; "for peanuts"

Examples: „Das bekommst du für einen Apfel und ein Ei."
"You can buy this for peanuts."

„Damals hat das nur einen Apfel und ein Ei
gekostet!"
"Back then it only cost peanuts!"

---

33. Jemanden auf die Palme bringen

Literally: to bring someone on the palm tree

Meaning: to make someone angry; "to drive somebody up
the wall"

Examples: „Das bringt mich auf die Palme!"
"That's driving me up the wall!"

„Du kannst einen wirklich auf die Palme bringen!"
"You can really make one angry!"

„Lass dich von ihm nicht auf die Palme bringen."
"Don't let him make you angry."

34. EIN AUGE AUF JEMANDEN/ETWAS WERFEN

Literally: to throw an eye on someone/something

Meaning: to check sb./sth. out

Examples: „Er hat ein Auge auf sie geworfen."
              "He checked her out."

              „Ich werde ein Auge auf den Text werfen."
              "I will have a look at this text."

35. ETWAS AUS DER NASE ZIEHEN

Literally: to pull sth. out of the nose

Meaning: to put effort in making someone talk; "it's like
             pulling teeth";
             "to have to worm sth. out of sb."

Examples: „Lass dir doch nicht alles aus der Nase ziehen!"
             "Don't make me worm everything out of you!"

             „Er redet nie, man muss ihm jedes Wort aus der
             Nase ziehen."
             "He never talks, you have to worm every word out
             of him."

---

36. QUATSCH MIT SOßE

Literally: nonsense with dip (sauce)

Meaning: "That's nonsense!"; "That's rubbish!"; "That's
             bullshit!"

Examples: „Glaub das nicht! Das ist doch Quatsch mit Soße!"
             "Don't believe that! That's nonsense!"

             „Die Geschichte ist Quatsch mit Soße! Alles
             gelogen!"
             "That story is rubbish! Only lies!"

37. Dumm/Blöd aus der Wäsche gucken

Literally: to look dumb out of the laundry

Meaning: "to look stupid/to look like an idiot" because
              something didn't work out as intended; You are
              surprised that it didn't work out;
              "to look a proper Charlie"

Examples: „Da hat er aber dumm aus der Wäsche geguckt!"
              *"He looked like a complete fool!" (He was also
              surprised by whatever happened.)*

              „Wir hätten ganz schön blöd aus der Wäsche
              geguckt."
              "We would have looked like a couple of fools."

---

38. Jemandem auf der Nase herumtanzen

Literally: to dance around on someone's nose

Meaning: to be cheeky; "to act up with somebody"

Examples: „Lass dir von ihr nicht auf der Nase herumtanzen!"
              "Don't let her act up with you!"

              „Musst du jedem auf der Nase rumtanzen?"
              "Do you really have to act up with everybody?"

              „Er tanzt seiner Mutter immer auf der Nase rum!
              "He always acts up with his mother!"

Note: "Rum" is often used instead of "herum" to make it shorter.

39. Einen Kater haben - verkatert sein

Literally: to have a tomcat; to be "tomcatted"

Meaning: to be hungover

Examples: *„Er hat gestern zu viel getrunken. Jetzt hat er einen Kater."*
"He drank too much yesterday. He's hungover now."

„Ich bin ziemlich verkatert."
"I'm pretty hungover."

40. Dahin gehen, wo der Pfeffer wächst

Literally: Going where the pepper grows

Meaning: to want somebody to go and stay away; "Get
              lost!"; "Go jump in a lake!"

Examples: „Geh doch hin, wo der Pfeffer wächst!"
              "Get lost!"

              „Sie kann dahin gehen, wo der Pfeffer wächst!"
              "She should get lost!"

---

41. Die beleidigte Leberwurst spielen

Literally: to play the offended liver-sausage

Meaning: someone who is easily offended, someone who is
              thin-skinned; "Sorehead"; "to get in a huff"

Examples: „Musst du immer die beleidigte Leberwurst
              spielen?"
              "Why do you always have to be such a
              sorehead?"

              „Sie spielt mal wieder die beleidigte Leberwurst."
              "She is getting in a huff again."

42. ALLES FIT IM SCHRITT?

Literally: Everything sporty in the crotch?

Meaning: Is everything okay?

Examples: *„Hi, wie geht's? Alles fit im Schritt?"*
              "Hi, how are you? Everything ok?"

              „Alles fit im Schritt bei dir?"- „Ja, alles fit im Schritt!"
              "Are you alright?"- "Yes, everything's ok!"

---

43. ACH DU GRÜNE NEUNE!

Literally: Oh, you green nine! (Neun/neune = 9)

Meaning: expression of surprise; "Good grief!"

Examples: *„Ach du grüne Neune! Was für ein Chaos!"*
              "Good grief, such chaos!"

              „Ach du grüne Neune, was ist denn hier passiert?"
              "Geeze, what happened here?"

44. Einen kühlen Kopf bewahren

Literally: to keep a cool head

Meaning: to keep a clear mind in a difficult situation; "to remain level-headed"; "to keep a cool head"

Examples: *„Du musst jetzt einen kühlen Kopf bewahren!"*
"You have to remain level-headed now!"

"In stressigen Situationen ist es schwierig einen kühlen Kopf zu bewahren."
"In stressful situations it is difficult to keep a cool head"

45. JEMANDEN VERMÖBELN

Literally: to furniture someone (die Möbel = the furniture)

Meaning: to beat somebody up

Examples: *„Er hat ihn ziemlich schlimm vermöbelt!"*
              "He beat him up quite badly!"

              „Das nächste Mal werde ich ihn vermöbeln."
              "Next time I will beat him up."

---

46. JEMANDEN AM ARSCH LECKEN (VULG.)

Literally: to lick somebody's ass/arse

Meaning: 1) Expression of surprise; "That's far out"
              2) Expression of rejection/denial; "Kiss my ass/arse!"

Examples: 1) *„Leck mich am Arsch, ist das geil[1]!"*
              "Wow, that's awesome!"

              2) *„Du kannst mich am Arsch lecken!"*
              "You can kiss my ass/arse!"

              „Leckt mich doch alle am Arsch!"
              "Kiss my ass/arse, all of you!"

Note: Often, we also say "Du kannst mich mal!", a short version of "Du kannst mich mal am Arsch lecken!"

TIP[1]: Germans use "geil!" to express that something is incredibly awesome. "Geil" is very common and used very often.

It can mean one of the two things: awesome or sexy. For example, when you say "Das Mädchen dort ist so geil" it's likely that you mean that she is hot/sexy. However, when something good happens and you yell „GEIL!!!", then it's likely that whatever happened is great/awesome.

Examples: „Das finde ich geil!"
              "I find that awesome!"

              „Die Reise war geil!" –
              "The trip was incredible!"

              „Ashton Kutcher ist geil!"
              "Ashton Kutcher is hot!"
              (Could also mean that he is awesome.)

But be careful, "geil" can also be "horny". So, "Ich bin geil!" can mean "I am awesome/sexy!" but also "I am horny!" depending on the context. ☺

---

47. Auf jemanden stehen

Literally: to stand on someone

Meaning: to have a crush on sb.; to be into sb.; to be attracted to sb.

Examples: „Ich steh' schon seit Jahren auf dich." (steh' = stehe)
               "I have fancied you for years."

               „Jeder weiß, du stehst auf ihn!"
               "Everyone knows, you are into him!"

„Er steht auf Männer."
"He is attracted to men."

Note: When you say "auf jemande**m** stehen" (with Dative) it means to stand on someone physically: *Ich stehe auf <u>dem Mann</u>. / Ich stehe auf <u>dir</u>.*

However, when you say "auf jemande**n** stehen" (with Accusative) it means to be into someone/to fancy someone: *Ich stehe auf <u>den Mann</u>. / Ich stehe auf <u>dich</u>.*

Are you starting to realize how important the 4 German cases are? ☺

48. 08/15 SEIN- ETWAS IST 08/15

Literally: to be 08/15; something is 08/15 (pronounced: Null -
                  Acht - Fünfzehn)

Meaning: something/someone is not special, average,
                  mediocre; It is used for unsatisfactory work and
                  products that lack quality, care, originality or
                  enthusiasm (like the tedious WWI machine gun drill,
                  after which it is named).

Examples: „Ich möchte keinen 08/15-Job!"
                  "I don't want a mediocre job!"

                  „Maya ist keine 08/15-Frau!"
                  "Maya is not an ordinary woman!"

                  "Räum dein Zimmer auf – aber nicht nur 08/15!"
                  "Clean up your room – but do it properly!"

---

49. DEN FINGER AUS DEM ARSCH ZIEHEN (VULG.)

Literally: to pull the finger out of the ass/arse

Meaning: a demand to act & stop hesitating; "Pull your finger
                  out!"; "Get off your ass."

Examples: „Jetzt zieh den Finger aus dem Arsch und mach
                  was!"
                  "Pull your finger out and do something!"

                  „Wann wird er den Finger aus dem Arsch ziehen?"
                  "When will he pull his finger out?"

50. Probieren geht über Studieren.

Literally: trying goes over studying

Meaning: it is more effective to do sth. than to study about
              how it is done;
              "The proof is in the pudding"; "Suck it and see!"

Examples: „Ich denke, in diesem Fall geht Probieren über
              Studieren."
              "I think in this case the proof is in the pudding."

              „Trau dich, sonst wirst du es nie wissen. Probieren
              geht über Studieren!"
              *"Take the plunge, otherwise you'll never know!
              Suck it and see!"*

---

51. Sich Kaputtlachen

Literally: to laugh oneself broken

Meaning: to laugh hard; "to crack up"; "to laugh oneself silly"

Examples: „Wir haben uns so kaputtgelacht!"
              "We were cracking up!"

              „Der Witz ist zum Kaputtlachen."
              "That joke is too funny for words."

52. DUMM WIE BROT

Literally: dumb as bread

Meaning: stupid person; "dumb as a rock/stump"; "thick as a brick"; "thick as two short planks"

Examples: *„Sie ist wirklich dumm wie Brot!"*
"She is really as dumb as a rock/stump!"

„Du bist dumm wie Brot!"
"You are as thick as a brick!"

53. Deutsche Sprache, schwere Sprache

Literally: German language, difficult language

Meaning: a phrase that is used ironically by native German speakers when it comes to German errors/mistakes

Examples: *„Wieso sagt man 'mit der Frau' obwohl es 'die Frau' ist?" - „Keine Ahnung! Ach ja, deutsche Sprache, schwere Sprache!"*
"Why do you say 'mit der Frau' when it is 'die Frau'?" - "I don't know. German is just a difficult language!"

---

54. Schmetterlinge im Bauch haben

Literally: to have butterflies in the stomach

Meaning: description of the exciting feeling in the belly when you are in love; "to have butterflies in the stomach"

Examples: *„Bist du verliebt? Hast du etwa Schmetterlinge im Bauch?"*
"Are you in love? Do you have butterflies in your stomach?"

„Verliebte Menschen haben Schmetterlinge im Bauch."
"People in love have butterflies in their stomach."

55. TOMATEN AUF DEN AUGEN HABEN

Literally: to have tomatoes on the eyes

Meaning: to not see the obvious

Examples: „Siehst du den Vogel nicht? Hast du Tomaten auf
                den Augen?"
                "Don't you see that bird? Are you blind?"

                „Anna hat Tomaten auf den Augen."
                "Anna doesn't see the obvious."

THE 20 FUNNIEST GERMAN WORD CREATIONS

With their literal translations, meanings and Sample Sentences

---

1. DIE FUßHUPE

Nomen/noun

Literally: the foot-horn (der Fuß = the foot, die Hupe = the horn)

Meaning: expression used for very small dogs

Examples: *„Hast du ihren neuen Hund gesehen? Eine Fußhupe ist das!"*
"Have you seen her new dog? It's a very small one!"

2. FUCHSTEUFELSWILD

Adjektiv/adjective

Literally: fox-devils-wild

Meaning: very furious; "hopping mad"

Examples: *„Das macht mich fuchsteufelswild!"*
"That drives me hopping mad!"

„Wenn sie das erfährt, wird sie fuchsteufelswild."
"When she finds out, she's going to be very angry."

---

3. DAS WEICHEI

Nomen/noun

Literally: the soft egg (weich = soft, das Ei = the egg)

Meaning: a wimpy person; "wuss"; "sissy"

Plural: die Weicheier (the soft eggs)

Examples: *„Du bist ein Weichei!"*
"You're a wuss!"

„Sei nicht so ein Weichei!"
"Don't be such a sissy!"

4. Das Flugzeug

Nomen/noun

Literally: the flight stuff (der Flug = flight, das Zeug = the stuff)

Meaning: the airplane

Plural: die Flugzeuge

Example: *„Siehst du das Flugzeug?"*
"Do you see the airplane?"

„Ich bin mit einem kleinen Flugzeug geflogen."
"I flew on a small airplane."

---

5. Das Arschgesicht (vulg.)

Nomen/noun

Literally: the ass/arse face (der Arsch = the ass, das Gesicht = the face)

Meaning: insult; "asshole"

Plural: die Arschgesichter

Examples: *„So ein Arschgesicht!"*
"What an asshole!"

„Sieh dir diese Arschgesichter an!"
"Look at these assholes!"

6. DIE NERVENSÄGE

Nomen/noun

Literally: the nerves-saw (der Nerv = the nerve, die Säge =
               the saw)

Meaning: an annoying person; "a nag"

Plural: die Nervensägen

Examples: „Sie ist eine richtige Nervensäge!"
               "She is a real nag!"

               „Ich bin von Nervensägen umgeben."
               "I am surrounded by nags!"

7. DAS FRÜHSTÜCK

Nomen/noun

Literally: the early piece (früh = early, das Stück = the piece)

Meaning: breakfast

Verb: frühstücken (to have breakfast)

Examples: *„Ich habe schon Frühstück gegessen."*
                "I've already had breakfast."

                „Wann gibt es Frühstück?"
                "When is breakfast?"

                „Was möchtest du frühstücken?"
                "What would you like to have for breakfast?"

                „Wir können zusammen frühstücken!"
                "We can have breakfast together!"

---

8. DER GESCHLECHTSVERKEHR

Nomen/noun

Literally: the gender-traffic (das Geschlecht = the gender,
                der Verkehr = the traffic)

Meaning: sex, sexual intercourse

Examples: *„Aus diesem Grund dürfen Sie keinen
                ungeschützten Geschlechtsverkehr haben."*
                *"Therefore, you must not have unprotected
                intercourse."*

                *„Hatten Sie mit all diesen Männern
                Geschlechtsverkehr? "*
                *"Did you have sexual intercourse with all of these
                men?"*

9. DER KLUGSCHEIßER (VULG.)

Nomen/noun

Literally: the smart shitter (klug = smart, scheißen = to shit)

Meaning: someone who thinks they know everything and is
            annoying because they correct everybody;
            "smartass"; "know-it-all"

Plural: die Klugscheißer

Verb: klugscheißen (smart-shitting)

Examples: *„Was für ein Klugscheißer!"*
            "Such a know-it-all!"

            „Du bist ein nerviger Klugscheißer!"
            "You are just an annoying know-it-all!"

            „Ich mag keine Klugscheißer."
            "I don't like know-it-all's."

10. DER DURCHFALL

Nomen/noun

Literally: the through-fall (durch = through, der Fall = the fall)

Meaning: diarrhea

Opposite: die Verstopfung = lit.: plugging/meaning: constipation

Examples: „Ich habe schon seit 2 Tagen Durchfall."
"I've had diarrhea for two days."

„Hast du oft Durchfall?"
"Do you often have diarrhea?"

„Durchfall haben nervt!"
"Having diarrhea is annoying!"

---

11. DER HANDSCHUH

Nomen/noun

Literally: the hand-shoe (die Hand = the hand, der Schuh = the shoe)

Meaning: the glove

Plural: die Handschuhe

Examples: „Im Winter trage ich immer Handschuhe."
"I always wear gloves in winter."

„Hast du meine Handschuhe gesehen?"
"Have you seen my gloves?"

„Mir fehlt ein Handschuh!"
"I am missing one glove!"

12. HERUMGURKEN/RUMGURKEN

Verb/verb

Literally: to cucumber around

Meaning: to drive around without knowing the destination, to
               drive around aimlessly

Examples: *„Ich bin zwei Stunden herumgegurkt bevor ich am
               Ziel war."*
               *"I drove around aimlessly for two hours before I
               arrived."*

               *„Ich erkundige mich nach dem Standort, bevor wir
               rumgurken!"*
               *"I will ask for the location, so we don't have to drive
               around aimlessly!"*

13. DAS STINKTIER

Nomen/noun

Literally: the stinky animal (stinken = to stink, das Tier = the animal)

Meaning: the skunk

Plural: die Stinktiere

Adjective: wie ein Stinktier = like a skunk

Examples: „Im Zoo haben wir Stinktiere gesehen."
                 "We saw skunks at the zoo."

                 „Du riechst wie ein Stinktier!"
                 "You smell like a skunk!"

---

14. DER SPARGELTARZAN

Nomen/noun

Literally: the asparagus-Tarzan
                 (der Spargel = the asparagus, Tarzan = Jungle-Man)

Meaning: very skinny (male) person; "beanpole"

Examples: „Früher war er ein Spargeltarzan."
                 "He used to be a beanpole."

                 „Komm doch her, du Spargeltarzan!"
                 "Come over here, you beanpole!"

15. Die Warteschlange

Nomen/noun

Literally: the waiting snake (warten = waiting, die Schlange = the snake)

Meaning: the queue, the line

Plural: die Warteschlangen

Examples: *„Die Warteschlange beginnt da hinten!"*
"The queue/line begins back there!"

„Die Warteschlange ist zu lang, ich gehe!"
"The queue/line is too long, I'm leaving!"

Tip: *Often we just use "Schlange" instead of "Wartschlange":*

„Vor der Sehenswürdigkeit war eine lange Schlange."
"There was a long queue/line in front of the sight."

16. DER STAUBSAUGER

Nomen/noun

Literally: dust-sucker (der Staub = the dust, saugen = sucking)

Meaning: the vacuum cleaner

Plural: die Staubsauger

Verb: staubsaugen (dust-sucking = to vacuum sth.)

Examples: *„Wo ist der Staubsauger?"*
"Where is the vacuum cleaner?"

„Ich habe einen neuen Staubsauger gekauft."
"I bought a new vacuum cleaner."

„Kannst du nachher staubsaugen?"
"Could you vacuum later?"

„Ich habe schon staubgesaugt."
"I've already vacuumed."

---

17. DIE BRUSTWARZE

Nomen/noun

Literally: the breast-wart (die Brust = the breast, die Warze = the wart)

Meaning: the nipple

Plural: die Brustwarzen

Examples: *„Jeder Mensch hat 2 Brustwarzen, außer ich: Ich habe 3."*
"Everybody has 2 nipples, except for me: I have 3."

„Meine Brustwarze schmerzt."
"My nipple hurts."

18. DIE PRESSWURST

Nomen/noun

Literally: the squeezed sausage (pressen = to squeeze, die Wurst = the sausage)

Meaning: a person who is wearing clothes that are too small/tight
("Presswurst": Sausage, that is pressed tightly in a can.)

Examples: *„Das Kleid ist zu klein, sie sieht aus wie eine Presswurst."*
"The dress she's wearing is too small, it looks like she's squeezed."

„Sehe ich in der Hose aus wie eine Presswurst? Ehrlich!"
"Do I look squeezed in these pants/trousers? Be honest!"

19. DAS ZAHNFLEISCH

Nomen/noun

Literally: the tooth-meat (der Zahn = the tooth, das Fleisch = the meat/the flesh)

Meaning: the gums

Examples: *„Das Zahnfleisch ist empfindlich."*
"The gums are sensitive."

„Mein Zahnfleisch ist oft entzündet."
"My gums are often inflamed."

---

20. DIE KLOBRILLE

Nomen/noun

Literally: the toilet-glasses (das Klo (coll.) = the toilet, die Brille = the glasses)

Meaning: the toilet seat

Plural: die Klobrillen

Examples: *„Mach bitte die Klobrille wieder runter!"*
"Please put the toilet seat back down!"

„I, eine dreckige Klobrille!"
"Ugh, a dirty toilet seat!"

„Klobrillen gibt es in vielen Farben und Formen."
"There are toilet seats in many colours and shapes."

BONUS: DIE NACKTSCHNECKE

Nomen/noun

Literally:	the naked snail (nackt = naked, die Schnecke = the snail)
Meaning:	the slug
Plural:	die Nacktschnecken
Examples:	*„Ich finde Nacktschnecken eklig."*
	"I find slugs disgusting."
	„Guck mal, eine Nacktschnecke!"
	"Oh look, a slug!"

DANKESCHÖN! THANK YOU!

Lieber Deutschlerner!

Thank you for reading my book. I'd love to hear your thoughts and reactions. If you liked this book, I'd highly appreciate it if you could leave a review on Amazon or contact me directly via my website www.learngermanwithanja.com if you have any suggestions for improvements or something similar!

If you know some funny expressions in the German language (there are so many!) and would like to put in your two cents, please email your expression suggestions to support@learngermanwithanja.com .

Deine Anja ☺

Made in the USA
Columbia, SC
08 November 2021